P9-DUK-058

READING POWER

Westward Ho!

THE MEXICAN-AMERICAN WAR

CONTRA COSTA COUNTY LIBRARY

EMILY RAABE

WITHDRAWN

The Rosen Publishing Group's
PowerKids Press™
New York

3 1901 03728 8075

Published in 2003 by The Rosen Publishing Group, Inc.
29 East 21st Street, New York, NY 10010

Copyright © 2003 by The Rosen Publishing Group, Inc.

All rights reserved. No part of this book may be reproduced in any form without permission in writing from the publisher, except by a reviewer.

First Edition

Book Design: Michael DeLisio

Photo Credits: Cover, pp. 6, 9, 11 © Bettmann/Corbis; p. 4 © Historical Picture Archive/Corbis; pp. 5, 12 Michael DeLisio; pp. 7, 18 © North Wind Pictures; p. 8 © Stock Montage/SuperStock; p. 13 © David Muench/ Corbis; pp. 14–15, 16–17, 19, 21 © Corbis; p.20 © Index Stock

Library of Congress Cataloging-in-Publication Data

Raabe, Emily.
The Mexican-American War / Emily Raabe.
  p. cm. — (Westward ho!)
Includes bibliographical references and index.
Summary: Describes the causes, progress, leaders, and results of the Mexican-American War.
ISBN 0-8239-6497-3 (library binding)
1. Mexican War, 1846-1848—Juvenile literature. [1. Mexican War, 1846-1848.] I. Title.
E404 .R16 2003
973.6'2—dc21
                                    2002001796

Contents

TROUBLE IN TEXAS

In 1824, the land now known as Texas became a part of Mexico. Both Americans and Mexicans lived there. In 1836, the people decided they wanted to be free from Mexico. They wanted to make their own laws. They formed the Republic of Texas.

Mexico City in 1832

Mexico City was the main city in Mexico.

The United States and Mexico in 1830

Mexico

United States

Present-day Texas

San Antonio

Mexico City

In 1830, present-day Texas was part of Mexico. Some Texans wanted to remain a part of Mexico. Some of them wanted to be free of Mexico. Others wanted to be part of the United States.

The leader of Mexico, General Santa Anna, did not want Texas to be free. In February 1836, Santa Anna and more than 1,800 soldiers attacked Texans at the Alamo in San Antonio, Texas. Santa Anna and his men killed everyone in the Alamo except for a few women and children and one slave.

Santa Anna

NOW YOU KNOW
Santa Anna left Susannah Dickerson alive at the Alamo so she could tell other Texans they would be killed if they fought against him!

Americans Jim Bowie and Davy Crockett were killed at the Alamo.

Freedom from Mexico

General Sam Houston led the Texans back into battle against Santa Anna. In April 1836, the Texans defeated Santa Anna and his troops along the San Jacinto *(SAN hah-SEEN-toe)* River near present-day Houston, Texas. The Texans had won their freedom from Mexico.

General Sam Houston

The Battle of San Jacinto lasted less than 30 minutes. Six Texans and about 600 Mexican soldiers were killed. Santa Anna (bowing) met with Sam Houston (lying down) after the battle.

President James Polk wanted more land for the United States. In 1845, he tried to buy the territories of New Mexico and California from Mexico. Mexico refused to sell this land. President Polk also wanted to make the Republic of Texas a part of the United States. In December 1845, Texas became a new state of the United States.

James Polk was the youngest president ever when he took office in 1845. He died three months after he left office in 1849.

Mexico was angry that Texas had become part of the United States. The two countries disagreed about the southern border of Texas. The United States said that the border between Texas and Mexico was the Rio Grande *(REE-oh GRAND)* River. Mexico said that it was the Nueces *(noo-AY-sehs)* River.

Mexico and Texas in 1845

United States

Texas

Nueces River

Rio Grande River

Mexico

Part of Texas claimed by Mexico

Texas became the 28th state of the United States in 1845.

The United States claimed the Rio Grande River was the border between Mexico and the United States.

13

Neighbors at War

President Polk sent John Slidell to Mexico to talk with officials about the Texas border. The Mexican government would not talk to Slidell. In April 1846, President Polk sent U.S. soldiers to the Rio Grande River in Texas.

The Mexican-American War began when Mexican and American soldiers fought along the Rio Grande River.

When Mexican troops attacked the American soldiers, the United States went to war against Mexico.

The United States was not only fighting Mexico to settle the Texas border claim, but also to get the New Mexico and California territories. Most people living in California wanted to be part of the United States.

In June 1846, American settlers in California started fighting the Mexican government. After several different battles, the United States gained control of California in January 1847.

One of the battles the U.S. Army fought against the Mexican government was in San Gabriel, California.

The War Ends

In September 1847, General Winfield Scott and 10,000 U.S. soldiers attacked Mexico City. After three days of fighting, General Santa Anna gave up. The Mexican-American War was over. It had lasted 16 months.

After the final battle of the Mexican-American War ended, General Scott and his men entered Mexico City.

General Winfield Scott was chosen to lead the last big battles against the Mexicans. Scott was very strict and was given the name Old Fuss and Feathers by his men.

After the war, Mexico and the United States signed an agreement called the Treaty of Guadalupe Hidalgo *(gwah-duh-LOO-pay ee-DAHL-goh)*. This treaty made the Rio Grande River the southern border of Texas. The Mexican-American War greatly changed the size of the United States.

Now You Know

The United States gave Mexico $15 million for the land it took over after the war.

The city of Houston, Texas, was named after Sam Houston, one of the U.S. generals in the Mexican-American War.

the respective Plenipotentiaries have signed this Treaty of Peace, Friendship, Limits and Settlement, and have hereunto affixed our seals respectively. Done in Quintuplicate at the city of Guadalupe Hidalgo on the second day of February in the year of our Lord one thousand eight hundred and forty eight

The Treaty of Guadalupe Hidalgo gave the United States the lands of present-day California, Nevada, Utah, and Texas; most of New Mexico and Arizona; and parts of Colorado and Wyoming.

21

Glossary

border (**bor**-duhr) the place where two countries, states, towns, or pieces of land meet

defeated (dih-**feet**-uhd) to have been beaten in a battle

republic (rih-**puhb**-lihk) a form of government in which the people choose their leaders

settlers (**seht**-luhrz) people who come to stay in a new country or place

territories (**tehr**-uh-tor-eez) the land and water that are controlled by a country or state

treaty (**tree**-tee) an agreement between two countries

Resources

Books

War with Mexico
by William Jay Jacobs
Millbrook Press (1993)

The Mexican War: Mr. Polk's War
by Charles W. Carey
Enslow Publishers (2002)

Web Sites

Due to the changing nature of Internet links, PowerKids Press has developed an online list of Web sites related to the subjects of this book. This site is updated regularly. Please use this link to access the list:

http://www.powerkidslinks.com/wh/meam/

Index

Word Count: 478

Note to Librarians, Teachers, and Parents

If reading is a challenge, Reading Power is a solution! Reading Power is perfect for readers who want high-interest subject matter at an accessible reading level. These fact-filled, photo-illustrated books are designed for readers who want straightforward vocabulary, engaging topics, and a manageable reading experience. With clear picture/text correspondence, leveled Reading Power books put the reader in charge. Now readers have the power to get the information they want and the skills they need in a user-friendly format.